power juices

50 energizing juices
and smoothies

**Penny Hunking
& Fiona Hunter**

The Authors

Penny Hunking is an Accredited Sports Dietitian and qualified fitness instructor. Penny is the author of two books about exercise and nutrition and is the Managing Director of Energise Nutrition, which aims to raise the awareness of good nutrition within an active lifestyle. She regularly appears on television and radio and contributes to a wide range of magazines.

Fiona Hunter has over 20 years' experience in the field of nutrition. In 1988 she became nutrition editor at *Good Housekeeping* magazine. She now works freelance contributing to a number of magazines and newspapers, as well as regularly appearing on television and radio.

First published in Great Britain in 2002 by Hamlyn, a division of Octopus Publishing Group Ltd
2–4 Heron Quays, London E14 4JP

Copyright © Octopus Publishing Group Ltd 2002

ISBN 0 600 60449 7

A CIP catalogue record for this book is available from the British Library

Printed and bound in China

10 9 8 7 6 5 4 3 2 1

contents

juices and smoothies in sport

Natural juices and smoothies are great for sports people because they deliver fluid, energy-giving carbohydrate and a wealth of other important nutrients all in one glass. They are quick and easy to prepare but, unlike most fast foods, they are packed full of vitamins and minerals and contain no artificial sweeteners, preservatives or other chemicals. All these factors make them attractive to sports people and the good news is that they will give a beneficial boost before, during and particularly after exercise (see page 19), a time when athletes can lose their appetite for solid food.

The need for fluid and carbohydrate is so important when exercising that it is better to consume carbohydrate in a less bulky, lower-fibre form, which makes it quicker and easier to absorb. Juices and smoothies fit the bill because they provide fluid and carbohydrate while being low in fibre. This is also convenient for athletes who have little time for eating and do not want too much bulky food when exercising – a juice is quick to drink and light on the stomach.

In addition, most sports people need to reach or maintain an appropriate body fat level and may need to monitor the amount of fat they eat. Juices and smoothies are generally low in fat and many of them are completely fat free.

key points

- Juices and smoothies provide valuable fluid, carbohydrate, vitamins (particularly the antioxidant vitamins C and E) and minerals.
- They provide vital nutrition before, during and after exercise – a particularly important time as the athlete may not be able to tolerate solid food.
- They are low in fat and in fibre (fibre slows carbohydrate absorption).
- Juices and smoothies can be high or low in energy as you wish, depending on your physical needs. See page 24 for the perfect juice or smoothie for each sport.
- Juices and smoothies are tasty, easy to make and ideal for sports people with limited time to prepare food.
- Home-made juices pack a nutritional punch. Not only do you avoid the vitamin and mineral losses that occur during cooking, but home-made juices are also free from preservatives, sweeteners and other chemicals, and provide a concentrated and easily absorbed source of vitamins and minerals.

Juicing basics

- Buy fruit and vegetables that are in season.
- Choose fruit that is ripe but not over-ripe.
- Avoid bruised or wilted produce.
- Whenever possible, buy organic (see page 22).
- Buy fruit and vegetables in small amounts and often.
- Prepare fruit and vegetables just before juicing, whenever possible, to retain the vitamins.

juices as supplements

Athletes often wonder what they can take to improve their performance. The use of nutritional supplements or ergogenic (work-producing) aids may help athletes towards their goal by:

- Making up for an inadequate diet or lifestyle.

what to juice

You can use almost any raw fruit or vegetables to make home-made juices and smoothies. While the flavour of some juices, especially those made from green vegetables, can take a little getting used to, apple, carrot, red pepper and citrus fruits are usually an instant success.

which fruit and vegetables are best for athletes?

Recent research has shown that some have a higher oxygen radical absorbency capacity (ORAC) than others. This measures their antioxidant potential – in other words, their ability to neutralize the damaging free radicals that can cause cancer and heart disease. Fruit with the highest ORAC are: prunes, blueberries, blackberries, strawberries, raisins, raspberries, oranges, plums, black grapes and cherries. Vegetables with the highest ORAC are: kale, red peppers, brussels sprouts, garlic, sweetcorn, spinach, onions, broccoli, aubergines and alfalfa.

- Meeting a specific or unusual nutrient requirement resulting from the demands of training and competition.
- Directly affecting sports performance.

A dietary supplement can be a number of different things, including:
- Sports drinks.
- High-carbohydrate supplements.
- Liquid meal supplements.
- Sports bars/energy bars.
- Vitamin and/or mineral supplements.
- Iron supplements.
- Calcium supplements.

Ergogenic aids contain nutrients in amounts greater than the recommended daily intake (RDI) and suggest or claim a direct effect on sports performance.

Yet there is little documented scientific support for many of these products. Some nutritional supplements do have a role in helping athletes train and perform better, but they can never be a substitute for a well-planned diet and training programme, adequate rest and recovery and good mental preparation.

Juices and smoothies are ideal supplements to the diet as they offer a host of nutrients that are easily absorbed and used by the body. By making them an integral part of your daily training diet, they will not only have a positive effect on your sports performance because of their high carbohydrate and fluid content; they will also contribute to your overall good health due to their high nutritional value.

5

sports nutrition

The right diet combined with proper training can significantly improve athletic performance, whether it's a Sunday morning football match or running a marathon. Exercise puts extra demands on the body – athletes need more energy, lose more body fluid and have extra stresses on muscles, bones and joints. Dietary changes can significantly affect training and recovery at every level. However, nutritional requirements vary widely – those who regularly train for more than one hour each day have different needs from those who enjoy a weekly team match.

So how do we know what to eat? Generally, energy intake increases during exercise, so food and drink choices must reflect this, while regulating the body's intake of macronutrients (protein, fat and

micronutrients of significant importance

Micronutrient	Function	Benefit to the athlete
Calcium	Bone/tooth structure. Helps muscle contraction, nerve transmission, secretion of hormones, digestive enzymes and neurotransmitters	Adequate calcium intake plus exercise prevents bone loss. Good bone health is essential and athletes need to be free from stress fractures and serious bone injury
Iron	Red blood cell formation. Transport of oxygen. Helps immune function	Iron deficiency can impair performance, both in training and competition. Exercise can destroy red blood cells, so sports people are likely to need more iron in their diet. Female athletes are particularly at risk because of menstrual blood losses
Vitamin A (retinol)	Essential for vision, especially at night. Protects mucous membranes lining the nose, mouth and throat, and so prevents bronchitis	Good vision is important to everyone, particularly sports people and those who train in low light
Vitamin C (ascorbic acid)	Growth and repair of cells and tissues. Promotes healthy blood vessels, gums and teeth. Powerful antioxidant	Exercise may increase vitamin C requirement. Vitamin C may help prevent cancer and heart disease
Vitamin E	Powerful antioxidant, protects from free radical damage	Protects cells from damage. Exercisers may need more than non-exercisers
Magnesium	Involved in muscle contraction and formation of new cells. Assists in energy production. Part of structure of bones	May play important role in aerobic metabolism
Zinc	Helps immunity. Involved in wound healing, metabolism of carbohydrates, proteins and fats. Vegetarian diets may be deficient in zinc	Adequate intake is important as sports people with a deficiency may have an impaired immune system
B vitamins	Many functions, including energy release from carbohydrates. Red blood cell formation. Manufacture of hormones and antibodies. Metabolism of fats, carbohydrates and proteins. Normal functioning of nerves, brain and muscles	May have increased needs related to energy production. Also involved in red blood cell formation so protects against anaemia

the principles of sports nutrition

- **To provide basic nutrient requirements**
- **To promote long-term good health**
- **To achieve and maintain appropriate levels of body mass and body fat**
- **To promote optimal recovery from training sessions**
- **To support training sessions**
- **To create opportunities to try out new eating and drinking practices**

Good sources

Milk, yogurt, cheese, canned fish with bones, baked beans, dried figs, oranges, apricots, green vegetables, sesame seeds, almonds, brazil nuts

Red meat, liver, lentils, fortified breakfast cereals, green leafy vegetables, figs, dates, beans, dark poultry meat

Liver, eggs, meat, whole milk, cheese, oily fish, margarine

Fruit and vegetables, particularly kiwifruit, citrus fruit, red peppers, strawberries and blackcurrants

Wholemeal bread, cereals, egg yolk, nuts, avocado, sunflower seeds

Fruit and vegetables, milk, potatoes, cereals

Milk and dairy products, eggs, meat, wholegrain cereals

Many, including brown rice, liver, nuts, eggs, pulses, green vegetables, bread, cereals, meat, chicken, turkey, offal, wheatgerm

carbohydrate) and micronutrients (vitamins, minerals and trace elements). There are about 20 different vitamins, most of which must be obtained from the diet. Vitamins A, D, E, K and B12 can be stored by the body; the rest need to be provided by the diet on a regular basis.

With the right food choices, most exercisers will automatically get more than enough nutrients in their diet. Juices and smoothies are a quick and easy way of ensuring a greater intake of essential nutrients, benefiting energy levels and long-term good health.

To acknowledge this link between diet and athletic performance, a whole new area of nutrition – sports nutrition – has evolved. Sports nutrition can be defined as: 'The influence of nutrition on human performance during the preparation for, the participation in and the recovery from sport and exercise.' (Professor Clyde Williams, Loughborough University.)

The main aims of sports nutrition are to help the athlete avoid fatigue, dehydration and poor performance, and to optimize his or her energy levels – the greater the intensity of the exercise, the greater the reliance on carbohydrate as a fuel. The two key issues are, therefore, carbohydrate intake and fluid intake.

vegetarian athletes

Vegetarians – whether they are athletes or not – usually have high-carbohydrate diets (bread, rice, pasta, cereals, potatoes and pulses). Vegetarian diets can be healthy since many vegetarians have a lower saturated fat intake than non-vegetarians. However, unless a vegetarian diet is balanced, it can lead to a deficiency in iron, vitamin B12, calcium, zinc and protein, so these nutrients are crucial.

the importance of carbohydrate

Carbohydrates are essential for optimum athletic performance, and the great news is that juices and smoothies are an excellent way to help you obtain the amount of carbohydrate you need every day.

After digestion, carbohydrate is either circulated in the blood as glucose where it is available for instant use, or stored in the liver and muscles as glycogen. Fatigue is associated with depletion of

7

glycogen stores, so athletes must eat sufficient carbohydrate to train and compete effectively.

The body stores only small amounts of carbohydrate and these decrease with any activity. It is important, therefore, to restock glycogen stores after training or you will experience a feeling of heavy legs and tiredness, particularly in endurance training, sprint training and team sports such as tennis, football, rugby and hockey.

Sources of carbohydrate

Sports people are usually told to eat more bread, rice, pasta, cereals and potatoes to get the energy they need, yet beans, pulses, fruit, some vegetables and dairy foods such as milk and yogurt also provide good levels of carbohydrate. Different sports place different demands on the participant, so food and drink should be matched to individual requirements (see page 14).

Glycaemic index

The glycaemic index ranks foods according to their effect on blood sugar – a food with a high glycaemic index causes blood sugar to rise more quickly than a food with a low glycaemic index.

Consumed after exercise, a high glycaemic index food will help to replace glycogen more quickly and may be useful during sport. A low glycaemic index food eaten before exercise, on the other hand, can provide a slow release of energy and help delay fatigue. Juices and smoothies vary in their glycaemic indices, depending upon the recipe and type of fruit and vegetables used (see individual recipes).

Foods with a high glycaemic index include: glucose, baked potato, watermelon, white bagels, honey and cornflakes.

Foods with a low glycaemic index include: milk, yogurt, oats, porridge, heavy-grain bread, apples, pears, plums, oranges, lentils and many soft fruits.

How much carbohydrate do athletes need?

This varies, depending on the type of exercise, its duration and how often it is performed. Clearly, the amount of carbohydrate needed also depends on body weight.

For weight maintenance, sedentary people require 4.5 g of carbohydrate per kilogram of body weight each day; active people require up to 10 g of carbohydrate per kilogram of body weight each day.

To determine your own carbohydrate needs, multiply your weight in kilograms (kg) by the appropriate amount of carbohydrate per kg from the table below. For example, a female athlete weighing 50 kg and training for more than one hour every day would require at least 300 g of carbohydrate daily

carbohydrate requirements of athletes

Training hours each day	Carbohydrate per kg body weight needed per day
less than 1 hour	4–5 g
1–2 hours	6–7 g
more than 3 hours	8–10 g

protein requirements of athletes

Type of athlete	Protein per kg body weight needed per day
Endurance/extra energy	1.2–1.4 g
Strength and power	1.4–1.8 g

(50 x 6 = 300 g). The recipes in this book are analysed to give their carbohydrate content.

fat

While some fat is essential in the diet – it provides the body with nine calories of energy per gram, plus the fat-soluble vitamins A, D, E and K – athletes should keep their fat intake to 30 per cent or less of their total calorie consumption. It is carbohydrate availability, not fat, that influences physical performance.

Sources of fat

Foods high in fat include butter, margarine, lard, oils, ghee, suet, fat on meat and skin on poultry, eggs, meat products, fried foods, chips, crisps, peanut butter, cakes, biscuits, mayonnaise and creamy sauces. Many ready-made meals and take-aways can also be high in fat. Not all fats are 'bad' and some are essential. Eat avocado, seeds, nuts and oily fish occasionally.

protein

Protein is needed for growth, repair and renewal of tissues, and reproduction. Each gram of protein provides the body with

four calories of energy, so proteins also provide energy when carbohydrates and fats are in short supply. Due to their increased energy intake and thus overall amount of food eaten, most athletes consume enough extra protein to compensate for their exercise.

The protein requirement for adults, as recommended by the World Health Organization, is 0.8 g of protein per kilogram of body weight per day. Animal proteins (such as meat, poultry, fish, cheese, eggs, milk and yogurt) are often quite high in fat. Vegetable proteins (such as peas, beans, lentils, bread, rice, cereals and potatoes), however, have a higher carbohydrate content and also provide energy. Other good sources of protein include nuts, seeds and soya products such as milk, cheese and yogurt.

fluid

A good fluid intake is essential for health and athletic performance – even mild dehydration can cause fatigue and affect performance. Start exercise well hydrated, drink fluids during exercise and replace fluids after exercise.

fluid losses

The amount of fluid lost during exercise depends on various factors, including the outside temperature, clothing and the intensity and duration of the exercise. In some activities, such as weight-training, glycogen is lost from the working muscle but the sweat rate may be quite low. Fluid and glycogen replacement becomes a priority when the recovery rate must be fast, for example, during competition over several days (particularly in the heat).

Fluid losses are measured as weight losses. Every kilogram of body weight lost during exercise reflects a loss of about 1.5 litres

(2½ pints) of fluid which must be replaced. A two per cent loss of body weight can affect performance and a four per cent loss of body weight can cause exhaustion. To determine how much has been lost, athletes should weigh themselves before and after exercise (preferably almost naked as sweat-soaked clothes are heavy) then compare results. To calculate your percentage body weight loss use this formula:

pre-exercise weight – post-exercise weight x 100
= percentage weight lost
For example:
60 kg – 58.5 kg x 100
= 2.5 per cent

what type of fluid?

Electrolytes are mineral salts that are dissolved in the body's fluids and are vital to help athletes maintain the water balance in their bodies. They also help muscles to contract and relax and transmit nerve impulses. To improve performance and to rehydrate after exercise, drinks that contain carbohydrate together with electrolytes, particularly sodium, are more effective than water alone. This is because they decrease urine production and aid fast rehydration and refuelling of

how do I store juices to go to the gym?

To store juices and especially smoothies, which usually contain dairy products, use a vacuum flask or a small ice box or cool bag and keep them refrigerated as much as possible. Drink juices and smoothies as soon as you can after making them, so that nutrient losses are minimized.

glycogen stores. In addition, water may quench the thirst before the exerciser has consumed enough fluid to replace losses. So drinks which contain electrolytes may be a better choice than plain water, especially for athletes who sweat heavily. Drinks fall into three categories – hypotonic, isotonic and hypertonic.

Hypotonic

Less concentrated than the body's fluids, these are quickly absorbed so they are useful both before and during exercise. Hypotonic drinks usually contain less than 4 g of carbohydrate in 100 ml fluid.

Isotonic

These have the same concentration of dissolved particles as the body's fluids and usually contain 4–8 g of carbohydrate in 100 ml. They can be drunk before, during and after exercise and are generally considered the best choice because they provide the exerciser with fluid and carbohydrate, yet are rapidly absorbed by the body. They can rehydrate and offset

potential dehydration better than hypotonic drinks. In addition, they supplement the body's limited carbohydrate stores and can improve exercise performance as well as preventing dehydration.

Hypertonic

These drinks have a higher concentration of dissolved particles than the body's fluids and are absorbed quite slowly, so are usually recommended after exercise when fluid replacement is not a priority. A hypertonic drink contains more than 8 g of carbohydrate in 100 ml.

key points

Hypotonic and isotonic drinks are absorbed quickly, so are useful when fast rehydration is needed usually before or during exercise. Hypertonic drinks are absorbed more slowly so these are a better choice when recovery can be slower and the priority is glycogen replacement, particularly if the athlete does not feel hungry. This is very important to remember when choosing a juice or smoothie for sports performance and recovery.

nutrition for long-term good health

Athletes need to keep up fluid and energy levels day to day, but they also need to think about their health in the long term. Exercise strengthens bones, but too much exercise and too little of the right food can seriously damage bones, particularly in women. Juices and smoothies provide many of the vitamins and minerals essential for long-term good health. Nutrition experts worldwide agree that fruit and vegetables are the cornerstones of a healthy diet – in Mediterranean countries, where fruit and vegetables form a large part of the diet, people are generally healthier. It is also known that fruit and vegetables can help protect against cancer, heart disease and many other health problems.

calcium

Essential for good bone health and also involved in nerve transmission, blood clotting and muscle function, calcium is found in milk and most dairy products, green leafy vegetables, canned fish with bones, nuts, seeds and fortified soya products

such as tofu. The absorption of calcium is aided by vitamin D, which we make ourselves by the action of sunlight on the skin.

Most of the juices in this book will boost your calcium intake. Smoothies made with milk, yogurt and ice cream can be very helpful in increasing calcium intake for athletes as this calcium is very easily available for use by the body.

Adequate calcium intake reduces the risk of osteoporosis, which can occur in young women, particularly if they over-exercise and are underweight with low body fat.

iron

An adequate intake of iron is essential for all athletes,

particularly females. Iron makes haemoglobin in the red blood cells that carry oxygen around the body. Even a marginal deficiency of iron can leave athletes too tired to train and recover effectively, with symptoms of severe fatigue, cramps, headaches and shortness of breath. Iron can be lost through sweat, gastro-intestinal bleeding and jarring during contact sports. Athletes who restrict how much they eat put themselves at a higher risk of developing iron deficiency.

Iron also helps in the synthesis of enzymes, forms part of the myoglobin in muscle cells and helps immune function. Iron from animal sources (red meat, for example) is absorbed in the body more easily than iron from vegetable sources, such as spinach. Iron absorption can be increased by eating foods rich in vitamin C (see recipes and Top Ingredients for Power Juices, page 20) at the same time as the

iron-rich foods. Iron deficiency is easily preventable by eating more iron-rich foods (green leafy vegetables, for example).

Sports anaemia

Sports anaemia, characterized by tiredness, is caused by an increased volume of blood in the body at the start of physical activity and means that iron is, in effect, more diluted in the blood. Performance is not generally affected, so if tiredness continues it is more likely to be due to a true lack of iron in the diet or another aspect of training. Self-diagnosis is not advised; if tiredness continues, see your doctor.

female athlete triad

This refers to three inter-related conditions: disordered eating, amenorrhoea (lack of menstruation) and osteoporosis.

Some female athletes and non-athletes do not consider that training or exercise is sufficient to achieve their ideal body shape. Consequently, a significant number use harmful practices such as restricted eating, vomiting, laxatives and diuretics to lose weight and shape up. These may lead to menstrual dysfunction, which in turn may cause reduced bone density and osteoporosis. Every portion of the triad increases the chance of ill health and death, but the dangers of the three together are synergistic.

Prevention is the only long-term solution: eat a healthy balanced diet that is sufficient in energy and contains a wide variety of foods.

when making smoothies, which has the most calcium – milk, yogurt or soya milk?
Both milk and yogurt are excellent sources of calcium. If you want to use soya milk, choose one that is enriched with calcium. The breakdown is as follows:

Product	Calcium per 100 ml
Full-fat milk	115 mg
Semi-skimmed milk	120 mg
Skimmed milk	120 mg
Calcium-enriched soya milk	120 mg
Yogurt	200 mg

13

high, particularly on hot days. Juices, smoothies and water are ideal to drink before and, indeed, throughout the game whenever the rules of the sport allow. Extra-energy sports include:

- Tennis
- Hockey
- Football
- Rugby
- Squash
- Circuit training
- Full-contact martial arts
- Water skiing (competition)
- Basketball
- Netball

Tennis Food and drink can be consumed between sets. Fluid needs can be very high and it is vital to drink as often as possible. Isotonic drinks are best: they replace lost fluids quickly and provide extra energy in the form of carbohydrate.

Hockey Recovery between matches is difficult, particularly with a heavy training load, and players must pay special attention to their intake of carbohydrate and fluid every day of the week. To maintain their weight, players should keep their general nutrient intake well balanced and follow a high-carbohydrate, low-fat eating style.

Football Footballers need a high level of fitness and energy. Some players have higher energy needs than others depending on their role and can experience fatigue quite early in the match. Good nutrition strategies help prevent this. The key is to keep carbohydrate and fluid intake high.

Rugby Forwards require strength and power to help win the ball through scrummages, rucks, mauls and strong tackles; backs help to carry the ball forward via their speed and agility to withstand the tackles from the opposition. Causes of fatigue in rugby players can be many – depletion of muscle glycogen stores and dehydration are the most likely.

Squash Squash is very demanding physically, requiring agility, coordination and good aerobic fitness. A match can last 90 minutes or more, with very high body temperature and sweat rates. Players must start a game well fuelled and well hydrated.

Circuit training Very intense exercise in which a group of exercises are completed one after another for a specific length of time. Many athletes use circuit training to complement training in their specific sport. Anyone circuit training should follow the principles of a well-balanced diet at all times.

Full-contact martial arts Training involves short bursts of energy, some of it very intense. Good technique is needed and good concentration is essential. Training sessions are often around two hours and an adequate fluid intake is key, especially among those who use diuretics and saunas for weight control. Athletes practising this sport may have increased iron needs because of bruising and bleeding from injuries (see box below).

Water skiing (competition, tricks) An extremely high-energy explosive sport that burns fuel and calories. In essence, water skiers hang around all day and then participate in several short intermittent periods of high-intensity exercise. It is vital they eat and drink regularly throughout the day. Fluid needs vary and could be very high on hot, sunny days.

which juices and smoothies are the best source of iron?

Many vegetables and fruit provide some iron, but not nearly as much as, say, red meat, dried fruit and dark green leafy vegetables. However, nearly all the fruit-based juices and smoothies in this book, especially those containing kiwi fruit, citrus fruits, peppers and watercress, are rich in vitamin C and this helps the body to absorb iron from other, iron-rich foods eaten at the same time.

Basketball Basketball requires a very high level of skill and fitness. Lower body fat levels can be an advantage to help jumps, speed and agility. Iron needs are likely to be higher because of the impact involved in contact with other players and impact on the floor. Fluid losses through sweating can be significant, so fluids must be consumed on the court sidelines.

Netball Netballers have similar needs to basketball players. Iron needs may be higher because of impact from running and jumps. There is increased destruction of red blood cells in athletes with high training loads of high-impact exercise. Fluid needs can be quite high, so fluids must be consumed on the court sidelines.

muscular strength activities

Many elite athletes and recreational exercisers weight-train, and these tough training sessions must be supported by high-energy intakes of carbohydrate. Protein is not as suitable as it is commonly thought since it is not converted into muscle, simply into extra energy to fuel the muscle. This extra energy is better obtained through carbohydrates. Muscle burns calories so athletes with more muscle need plenty of energy. They should eat regularly and keep well hydrated. Juices and smoothies are an ideal way of achieving this.

general fitness activities

What is fitness? It is a relative term with many health-related and skill-related components. Health-related components include muscular strength and endurance, aerobic fitness and flexibility. Skill-related components include balance, agility, reaction time, speed, power and coordination. General fitness activities include:

- Gym workouts
- Pilates
- Yoga
- Body conditioning
- Water skiing
- Wakeboarding
- Sailing
- Roller skating
- Skateboarding
- Semi-contact martial arts
- Hiking
- Ice skating
- Playing with a Frisbee
- Housework, gardening, washing the car
- Walking the dog

eating and competing

Anyone who exercises regularly must follow a well-balanced, nutrient-dense diet, matching energy intake and expenditure to achieve a consistent weight. Fluid intake is of key importance: even a small amount of dehydration affects balance, coordination, agility and concentration, impairs performance and can lead to fatigue.

What the athlete actually needs in theory may be difficult to achieve in practice. Carbohydrate and fluid intakes are the most important considerations and juices and smoothies can deliver both at the same time and in an easily tolerated form. The key to eating and competing is to practise different eating and drinking strategies until you find one that suits you personally. Do not try anything new 'on the day' or you could experience a few undesirable side effects!

before the event

Some athletes can eat and compete, some cannot. The pre-event meal – two to three hours beforehand – should be high in carbohydrate and low in fat and should be easy to digest so the stomach is left empty for the event. Remember that liquid meals will empty from the stomach quickly, so you may need more to sustain yourself over a longer period of time. Ask yourself the following questions:

- Does the event involve running, jumping or physical contact?
  If so, leave a little longer between eating and competing.
- Is your body supported – for example, cycling, swimming and rowing?
  If so, you may be able to eat nearer the event.
- Will you get an attack of nerves?
  If so, eat a little earlier.

during the event

Nutritional and fluid needs vary widely, although studies show that carbohydrate intake during prolonged exercise lasting longer than 90 minutes enhances performance. Fluid intake before, during and after an event is a priority. Juices and smoothies are very useful because they:

- Taste good, so more is likely to be drunk.
- Are easy to absorb.
- Deliver some carbohydrate to help improve endurance and delay fatigue.

Unfortunately, many athletes suffer from nausea, vomiting and diarrhoea during competitive events. Problems often relate to the pre-event meal, so juices and smoothies may be more suitable than solid food.

Factors that increase the risk of problems are:
- Poor training
- Dehydration
- Nervousness
- Being female
- High-intensity exercise
- Running and jumping

Team sports

Most team sports last up to about 90 minutes. Players need to start the game with well-fuelled muscles, so they should eat plenty of food and drink containing carbohydrate. During the game or event, an isotonic drink will help to replace fluid lost in sweat and provide some carbohydrate to delay fatigue.

Endurance events

Endurance events usually last longer than 90 minutes and so it is important to take on fluid and

---

pre-event juices and smoothies

Juices and smoothies are especially suitable before an event if:
- **You are not hungry**
- **The event starts very early**
- **The event involves running, jumping or physical contact**
- **Fluid replacement is a priority**
- **It is a hot and/or humid day**

is there any difference between juices and smoothies for athletes?

Your choice will depend largely on fluid needs and personal preference – find juices and smoothies that suit you. Smoothies, full of nutrients and a good source of calcium, are usually more filling and a good choice before and immediately after exercise when solid food may not appeal to you. Juices also provide a wealth of nutrients, but are often useful during exercise when fluid needs are higher. Choose an isotonic juice or smoothie when fluid replacement is important.

Smoothies contain both carbohydrate and protein, and are therefore ideal to help rehydration and refuelling of the muscles.

The first meal after exercise should provide at least 1 g of carbohydrate per kilogram of body weight. Athletes should also drink at least 500 ml (17 fl oz) of fluid immediately after competing and continue drinking at regular intervals.

fuel (carbohydrate) throughout. Smoothies would be ideal here, as they will provide fluid and the extra 30–60 g of carbohydrate needed. When sweat rates are high, the athlete should choose an isotonic drink.

Ultra-endurance events

These challenging events, such as Ironman triathlon, usually last over four hours and test the fuel supplies of the participants. These athletes compete at a lower intensity, so digestion is often little affected and athletes can eat, drink and digest food and fluids with higher carbohydrate during the event. Smoothies are ideal, together with snacks such as muesli bars and jam sandwiches.

after the event

The athlete may be too exhausted to even think about eating and drinking after competing, yet it is vital to do so as soon as possible – preferably within two hours of the completion of the event.

19

top ingredients for power juices

Apples have a higher antioxidant vitamin content than soft or citrus fruits as they contain a flavonoid called quercetin, thought to be a potent antioxidant. Exercisers may need extra antioxidants to counter the potentially damaging effect of free radicals, produced more freely during exercise.

Apricots, particularly dried, are a good source of beta-carotene, potassium and iron.

Avocados contain more protein than any other fruit, and are high in monounsaturated fat. They are a rich source of vitamin E and also supply reasonable amounts of vitamin C, vitamin B6, potassium, riboflavin and manganese.

Bananas are especially popular with endurance athletes as they are a great source of carbohydrate and potassium, but are low in fat and sodium. Make sure you choose really ripe ones as unripe bananas are largely indigestible.

Carrots are an excellent source of beta-carotene (made more available by juicing), the plant form of vitamin A, which is crucial for good vision – particularly useful for scuba divers and early-morning runners. High intakes of beta-carotene may also help to fight the damage done by free radicals and so protect against some types of cancer. Carrots can also help lower blood cholesterol levels.

Cranberries – daily consumption of cranberry juice helps to decrease the risk of urinary tract infections (UTIs). Cranberries are also a good source of antioxidant vitamin C and flavonoids.

Grapes are ideal after exercise as they are a good source of potassium. Red and black grapes contain more antioxidants than green ones.

Kiwifruits are naturally high in potassium and vitamin C, which helps to protect athletes from muscle damage, decreases muscle soreness and accelerates general healing. Vitamin C may also help to increase oxygen uptake and aerobic energy production which is particularly useful for athletes.

Lemons are an excellent source of vitamin C, an essential water-soluble vitamin involved in many metabolic processes including those that influence the functioning of the aerobic system. A very powerful antioxidant, vitamin C helps to prevent cellular damage and impairment of the immune system and aids the absorption of dietary iron.

Mangoes are an excellent source of vitamin C and beta-carotene, which is converted into vitamin A, boosting the body's defences and preventing damage by free radicals.

Melons are low in calories and high in water content. Orange-fleshed melons are a good source of vitamin C and beta-carotene; lighter-coloured melons less so. Watermelons have a high glycaemic index, so juices made with this fruit are good after exercise, particularly when fluid replacement is a priority.

Oranges are an excellent source of vitamin C, a powerful antioxidant. They also provide folate (important for female athletes) and potassium (vital for muscle and nerve function).

Peaches are an excellent source of vitamin C. They are easily digestible and have a gentle laxative effect.

Pears are a useful source of vitamin C and potassium. They contain natural fruit sugars for extra energy.

Pink grapefruits are a great source of vitamin C, folate (an essential B vitamin), potassium and lycopene. Folate deficiency could impair aerobic performance; it is also vital for females of child-bearing age because of its role in the prevention of birth defects.

Plums, particularly dried ones (prunes), contain useful amounts of fibre and are a good source of potassium. They also contain iron.

Purple grape juice contains favourable amounts of antioxidants called bioflavonoids and is a good source of potassium – essential for optimum cell, nerve and muscle

function and for regulating blood pressure, and therefore vital for athletic performance.

Redcurrants are an excellent source of vitamin C and a good source of potassium. They also contain reasonable levels of iron.

Spinach is a great source of beta-carotene (vitamin A) and a fair source of many other nutrients including iron, calcium, folate and vitamins B1, C and E.

Strawberries are a great source of vitamin C. In addition, they are a fair source of folate, which is also necessary for red blood cell manufacture and so is needed to prevent anaemia.

Tomatoes are a good source of vitamin C and the antioxidant, lycopene. Research indicates that people who frequently eat

21

is it nutritionally better to eat organic fruit and vegetables?

Organically grown produce may contain higher levels of vitamins and phytochemicals. But there is another reason for choosing organic produce. Unless you buy organic, you will inevitably increase your intake of pesticide residues. Although the health risks from pesticides are small, the effects of long-term exposure to them are unknown. However, some residues can be removed by thoroughly washing fruit and vegetables.

tomatoes and tomato products have a lower risk of certain cancers, particularly prostate cancer, and heart disease, than those who eat them rarely. Tomato-based juices are ideal before and after exercise.

Milk – athletes can achieve their required daily intake of calcium by drinking just 600 ml (1 pint) of milk daily. Ninety-nine per cent of the body's calcium is in the skeleton, making it essential for athletes who need strong, healthy bones. Milk is also a good source of protein, zinc, phosphorus, B vitamins and vitamin A. Skimmed milk loses its vitamin A, but is lower in fat than whole milk. Semi-skimmed and skimmed milk are a better source of calcium than whole milk.

Quark is a soft curd cheese which is low in fat and, like fromage frais, is an excellent source of protein, vitamins and minerals, including calcium.

Soya milk is an alternative to cows' milk for vegan or lactose-intolerant athletes. However, because soya milk naturally lacks calcium, it is better to choose a brand that is fortified with calcium. Soya milk contains about the same amount of protein as cows' milk and there is growing interest in the role that soya plays in men's and women's health.

Yogurt is a great source of calcium. It also has a low glycaemic index so is ideal before endurance exercise as well as after exercise.

Peanut butter – fibre-providing peanuts are more than 25 per cent protein and high in fat, although over 75 per cent of this is monounsaturated and polyunsaturated, which can help to reduce blood cholesterol levels. Peanut butter is a good source of vitamin E and B vitamins, copper and magnesium. Peanuts also contain phytochemicals including resveratrol, thought to play a role in protecting against cancer and heart disease.

fruit facts

- Fresh fruit – always use ripe, top-quality fruit and, wherever possible, buy organic
- Canned fruit – choose fruit canned in natural juice or water, rather than syrup
- Dried fruit – ready-to-eat apricots, prunes and dates are a concentrated source of sugars, vitamins and minerals. To make the fruit soft enough to purée, soak it in fruit juice overnight
- Frozen fruit – a good alternative to fresh fruit, particularly in the winter months. Using frozen fruit gives smoothies a thick, creamy consistency and helps them stay cold for longer (useful if you are taking them to the gym)

making perfect juices and smoothies

Refreshing and nutritious, juices and smoothies are quick and easy to prepare and make a great energy booster, snack or meal replacement. All you need is a sharp knife, a juice extractor and a blender or food processor.

equipment

If you plan to make both juices and smoothies you will need two machines. For juices you will need a juice extractor, for smoothies you will need a blender or food processor. Other useful items include a chopping board, a sharp knife and a scrubbing brush.

Choosing a juicer

The most basic juicer is an electronic citrus press which juices only citrus fruits. For other fruit and vegetables you will need a juice extractor. With these machines you get what you pay for, so if you are serious about juicing it is worth investing in the best machine that you can afford.

There are two main mechanisms for juicers: centrifugal and masticating. In centrifugal juicers, the juice and pulp are separated by centrifugal force. Masticating juicers mash the fruit and push it through a mesh. These tend to be

more expensive, but produce a larger quantity of juice.

understanding the nutrition notes in the recipes

RNI (Reference Nutrient Intakes) refer to the amount of a nutrient that is required to meet the nutritional needs of most people. They are equivalent to what used to be called Recommended Daily Amounts or Intakes (RDA/RDI).

key to recipe symbols

The quick-reference symbols beside each recipe indicate for which type of exercise the drink is most beneficial, and whether it is best enjoyed before, during or after exercise. The activity symbols are listed directly below the time symbols for which they are appropriate. For example on page 31, Carrot and Kiwifruit juice is best before general fitness and during aerobic and low-intensity exercise.

 pre-exercise

 aerobic exercise
(see page 14)

 extra-energy sports
(see page 15)

 during exercise

 endurance activities
(see page 14)

 muscular strength activities
(see page 17)

 post-exercise

 low-intensity exercise
(see page 15)

 general fitness
(see page 17)

23

which drinks for which sport?

This table shows which juices and smoothies are best before, during and after each type of exercise. The numbers refer to the pages on which the recipes can be found.

sport category	pre-exercise	during exercise	post-exercise
aerobic exercise fitness classes/aerobic, running, swimming, cycling (leisure), power walking, social dancing	pages: 28, 32, 36, 38, 40, 42, 44, 52, 54, 56, 60, 92, 104, 110, 116	pages: 28, 30, 32, 38, 40, 42, 52, 56, 60, 68, 70, 74, 76, 80, 104, 106	pages: 32, 36, 42, 44, 46, 48, 54, 58, 60, 66, 72, 78, 82, 88, 90, 92, 94, 102, 104, 106, 108, 110, 112, 114, 116, 118, 122, 124
endurance activities long-distance running, triathlon, rowing, competition swimming, cross-country running, cycling (racing)	pages: 32, 42, 46, 48, 50, 52, 54, 56, 60, 64, 66, 82, 84, 110, 116, 120	pages: 32, 42, 52, 56, 60, 62, 68, 74, 76, 98, 100, 120	pages: 32, 42, 48, 54, 58, 60, 62, 64, 66, 72, 78, 82, 84, 88, 90, 94, 98, 100, 102, 108, 110, 112, 114, 116, 118, 120, 122, 124
low-intensity exercise walking, golf, cricket, scuba diving	pages: 28, 34, 36, 38, 40, 42, 44, 58, 60, 92, 94, 104, 116, 118, 120	pages: 28, 30, 38, 40, 42, 60, 86, 96, 98, 100, 104, 106, 120	pages: 36, 42, 44, 60, 86, 92, 96, 98, 100, 104, 106, 116, 120

sport category	pre-exercise	during exercise	post-exercise
extra-energy sports tennis, hockey, football, rugby, squash, circuit training, full-contact martial arts, water skiing (competition), basketball, netball	pages: 32, 42, 44, 52, 54, 56, 60, 64, 84, 110, 116	pages: 32, 42, 52, 56, 60, 62, 68, 70, 74, 76, 80, 100	pages: 32, 42, 44, 46, 48, 54, 58, 60, 62, 64, 66, 72, 78, 82, 84, 88, 90, 94, 100, 102, 108, 110, 112, 114, 116, 118, 122, 124
muscular strength activities	pages: 42, 110, 120	pages: 42, 76, 120	pages: 42, 46, 66, 82, 90, 94, 102, 108, 110, 112, 114, 118, 120, 122, 124
general fitness activities gym workouts, Pilates, yoga, body conditioning, water skiing, wakeboarding, sailing, roller skating, skateboarding, semi-contact martial arts, hiking, ice skating, playing with a Frisbee, housework, gardening, walking the dog	pages: 28, 30, 32, 34, 36, 38, 40, 42, 44, 52, 54, 56, 60, 64, 84, 92, 104, 110, 116, 120	pages: 26, 28, 32, 38, 40, 42, 52, 56, 60, 68, 70, 74, 76, 80, 86, 98, 100, 104, 106, 120	pages: 26, 32, 36, 42, 44, 46, 48, 54, 58, 60, 64, 84, 86, 88, 92, 94, 98, 100, 102, 104, 106, 108, 110, 112, 116, 118, 120, 122

beetroot, apple and carrot

As beetroot has such a strong flavour it is best diluted, making it a great isotonic drink pre-, during or post-exercise. Vitamin C, folic acid and iron are all essential nutrients for athletes, making this juice a good choice for exercisers.

2 small beetroot
1 carrot
2 apples
300 ml (½ pint) water

Scrub the beetroot and carrot. Wash the apples. Cut all the ingredients into even-sized pieces and juice. Add the water, then pour into a glass, adding a couple of ice cubes. **Makes 600 ml (1 pint); Serves 2**

Nutrition Notes

Beetroot is high in oxalic acid and should be avoided by anyone with oxalate kidney stones. This juice is an excellent source of vitamins A, C, B1 and B6, folic acid, potassium and phosphorus, and provides useful amounts of iron.

Per serving

calories: 165
fat: 0.6 g
carbohydrate: 39 g
iron: 1.5 mg (10% RNI)
calcium: 53 mg (8% RNI)

33

celery, apple
and alfalfa

Although it provides good amounts of vitamins A, C and K, alfalfa is rather bitter on its own and needs to be combined, as here, with sweeter flavours. This juice is perfect pre-exercise, especially before general fitness activities such as gardening. Because it contains a good amount of folic acid, it is particularly beneficial to female athletes.

3 celery sticks
2 tart-flavoured apples, such as
* Granny Smith*
25 g (1 oz) alfalfa

Wash the celery and apples and cut into even-sized pieces. Rinse the alfalfa. Feed all the ingredients into a juicer in alternating batches. Pour into a glass, add a couple of ice cubes and drink immediately.
Makes 250 ml (8 fl oz); Serves 1

Nutrition Notes

This juice is an excellent source of vitamin C, B6 and potassium, and provides useful amounts of B1 and folic acid. Alfalfa, along with all other sprouted beans and seeds, is rich in vitamins B and C.

Per serving

calories: 106
fat: 0.6 g
carbohydrate: 24 g
iron: 0.8 mg (6% RNI)
calcium: 53 mg (8% RNI)

carrot, orange and apple

A delicious combination of flavours, this juice is a good source of vitamins and fibre. Apples contain pectin, a type of soluble fibre that can help reduce high blood cholesterol levels. This is a good choice for vegetarian athletes as the vitamin C from the oranges helps the body absorb iron, something that non-meat eaters often lack.

2 carrots, about 200 g (7 oz) in total
1 orange
1 tart-flavoured apple, such as
  Granny Smith

Scrub the carrots. Peel the orange and divide into segments. Cut the carrots and apple into even-sized pieces. Juice all the fruit, pour into a glass then add a couple of ice cubes. **Makes 250 ml (8 fl oz); Serves 1**

Nutrition Notes

Carrots are one of the richest sources of the antioxidant beta-carotene. This juice is an excellent source of vitamins C, B1 and B6, as well as folic acid and potassium. It provides useful amounts of calcium.

Per serving

calories: 160
fat: 0.8 g
carbohydrate: 38 g
iron: 0.8 mg (5% RNI)
calcium: 110 mg (16% RNI)

celery, tomato and red pepper

Ideal before general fitness activities, such as body-conditioning classes, this juice is an excellent source of vitamin C, which is involved in many of the body's metabolic processes, including those that are crucial for good functioning of the aerobic system. In addition, the vitamin C will aid the absorption of iron which is great for all athletes, particularly vegetarian athletes.

4 celery sticks
3 ripe tomatoes
½ red pepper
½ red chilli, deseeded (optional)
1 clove garlic, crushed (optional)

Cut the vegetables into even-sized pieces and juice. Pour into a glass, stir in the chilli and crushed garlic, if using, and add a couple of ice cubes, if liked.

Makes 300 ml (½ pint); Serves 1

Nutrition Notes

Weight for weight, red peppers contain over twice as much vitamin C as oranges. This juice is an excellent source of vitamins A, C, B1, B2 and B6, folic acid, potassium and phosphorus, and provides useful amounts of iron and calcium.

Per serving

calories: 83
fat: 1.4 g
carbohydrate: 15 g
iron: 2.2 mg (15% RNI)
calcium: 76 mg (11% RNI)

celery, tomato, lemon and parsley

This vibrant, fresh-tasting juice is packed full of nutrients. It provides 15% of our daily requirement of calcium, making it a good choice for all exercisers. For women athletes who may be prone to osteoporosis (brittle bone disease) it is a good drink to opt for before exercise. This juice is also an excellent source of iron, which is essential for athletes to prevent fatigue and anaemia.

2 celery sticks
4 tomatoes
large handful of parsley
rind and juice of ½ lemon

Wash the celery, tomato and parsley. Feed into the juicer in alternating batches, along with the lemon juice and zest. Pour the juice into a glass and add a couple of ice cubes. **Makes 300 ml (½ pint); Serves 1**

Nutrition Notes

Eaten in reasonable quantities, parsley can provide useful amounts of vitamin C, iron, calcium and potassium. Overall this juice is an excellent source of vitamins A, C, B1 and B6, niacin, folic acid, iron, potassium, phosphorus, magnesium and it also provides useful amounts of calcium.

Per serving

calories: 82
fat: 1.6 g
carbohydrate: 14 g
iron: 4 mg (28% RNI)
calcium: 104 mg (15% RNI)

41

pear and pineapple

A good drink to choose before or after most activities including extra-energy sports, such as circuit training and basketball. Pineapples contain an enzyme, bromelain, that breaks down protein. This juice is rich in B vitamins. These help release energy from carbohydrate – essential for all athletes, especially those who practise aerobic, endurance or extra-energy sports.

2 pears
¼ pineapple, about 215 g (7½ oz)
flesh once skin and core have
been removed
½ lime

Wash the pears. Remove the skin and hard central core from the pineapple. Scrub the lime. Chop the fruit into even-sized pieces and juice it. Pour into a glass and add a couple of ice cubes, if liked.
Makes 300 ml (½ pint); Serves 1

Nutrition Notes

This juice is an excellent source of vitamins C, B1 and B6, calcium and copper.

Per serving

calories: 212
fat: 0.8 g
carbohydrate: 53 g
iron: 1 mg (7% RNI)
calcium: 74 mg (10% RNI)

49

pear, kiwifruit and lime

Weight for weight, kiwifruits contain more vitamin C than oranges. Athletes often suffer muscle damage during training and, even with precautions, often seem to attract bangs, knocks and other injuries. Ensuring that there is enough vitamin C in your diet helps protect against muscle damage, and leads to a reduction in muscle soreness and improved general healing. Vitamin C may also help to increase oxygen uptake and aerobic energy production.

2 ripe pears
3 kiwifruits
½ lime

Wash the pears, peel the kiwifruits and scrub the lime. Slice the fruit into even-sized pieces then juice. Pour into a glass, add a couple of ice cubes and decorate with slices of pear, if liked. **Makes 300 ml (½ pint); Serves 1**

Nutrition Notes

This juice is an excellent source of vitamins C and B6, copper, magnesium and phosphorus and provides useful amounts of calcium.

Per serving

calories: 210

fat: 1.2 g

carbohydrate: 49 g

iron: 1.3 mg (9% RNI)

calcium: 78 mg (11% RNI)

watermelon
and raspberry

A refreshing juice that can be drunk at almost any time by most athletes. Watermelons are classed as having a high glycaemic index, so juices containing watermelon are good to drink during or after exercise to aid fast muscle refuelling, particularly when fluid replacement is a priority.

**¼ watermelon, about 300 g
(10 oz) flesh
125 g (4 oz) raspberries**

Remove the skin and seeds from the watermelon and chop the flesh into even-sized pieces. Juice the watermelon and raspberries, pour into a large glass and add a couple of ice cubes. **Makes 350 ml (12 fl oz); Serves 1**

Nutrition Notes

This juice is an excellent source of vitamins A, C and B1, folic acid, magnesium and phosphorus.

Per serving

calories: 125
fat: 1.3 g
carbohydrate: 27 g
iron: 1.8 mg (12% RNI)
calcium: 52 mg (8% RNI)

melon and grape

This isotonic juice is particularly suitable during extra-energy and endurance activities when a thirst-quenching drink is required. Grapes are a good source of potassium and make the perfect energy snack after these types of exercise.

½ Galia melon, about 300 g (10 oz)
175 g (6 oz) seedless green grapes
300 ml (½ pint) water

Remove the skin and the seeds from the melon and chop the flesh into even-sized pieces. Wash the grapes. Juice the fruit then add the water. Pour the juice into a glass and add a couple of ice cubes, if liked. **Makes 600 ml (1 pint); Serves 2**

Nutrition Notes

This juice is an excellent source of vitamins C, B1 and B6, copper, magnesium and phosphorus.

Per serving

calories: 180
fat: 0.5 g
carbohydrate: 44 g
iron: 1 mg (8% RNI)
calcium: 62 mg (9% RNI)

watermelon and orange

This is the perfect juice to drink before an endurance or extra-energy activity, or after general fitness sports. As well as copious amounts of vitamin C, it provides potassium, which is vital for muscle and nerve function during exercise. Watermelons have a high glycaemic index, making them ideal after exercise when fluid requirements are high and refuelling muscle stores is paramount.

¼ **watermelon, about 300 g (10 oz) flesh**
2 oranges

Remove the skin and seeds from the watermelon and chop the flesh into even-sized pieces. Peel the oranges and divide the flesh into segments. Juice the fruit, pour it into a glass and add a couple of ice cubes. Garnish with slices of orange, if liked.

Makes 300 ml (½ pint); Serves 1

Nutrition Notes

This juice is an excellent source of vitamins C and B6, folic acid, calcium, copper and potassium, which help provide energy and improve muscle and nerve function.

Per serving

calories: 200
fat: 1 g
carbohydrate: 47 g
iron: 1.2 mg (8% RNI)
calcium: 162 mg (23% RNI)

65

melon, kiwifruit and grape

This is a great juice to drink before an endurance event, when you want to fill your body with as many nutrients as possible, without drinking anything too heavy. It provides good amounts of calcium and carbohydrate. In addition, the large amount of vitamin C in kiwifruit protects against muscle damage, reduces muscle soreness and accelerates healing after injury.

375 g (12 oz) honeydew melon
2 kiwifruits
125 g (4 oz) seedless green grapes

Remove the skin and seeds from the melon. Peel the kiwifruits. Chop the melon and kiwifruits into even-sized pieces. Juice all the fruit, pour into a glass and add a couple of ice cubes. **Makes 300 ml (½ pint); Serves 1**

Nutrition Notes

This juice is an excellent source of vitamins C, B6 and B1, as well as copper, potassium, magnesium and phosphorus and also provides useful amounts of calcium, essential for healthy bones and bone strength, as well as protecting against osteoporosis.

Per serving

calories: 232
fat: 1 g
carbohydrate: 55 g
iron: 1.2 mg (8% RNI)
calcium: 78 mg (11% RNI)

67

orange and raspberry

This is an excellent isotonic drink containing plenty of calcium, which is great for drinking during endurance, extra-energy or general fitness activity, as it gives a good boost of vitamin C, plus potassium and folate. Folate is essential for women of child-bearing age because it helps protect against birth defects.

2 large oranges
175 g (6 oz) raspberries
250 ml (8 fl oz) water

Peel the oranges and divide the flesh into segments. Wash the raspberries. Juice the fruit then add the water. Pour into a glass and add a couple of ice cubes.
Makes 500 ml (17 fl oz); Serves 2

Nutrition Notes

This juice is an excellent source of vitamins C, B6 and B1, folate, zinc, copper, calcium and potassium and provides useful amounts of iron.

Per serving

calories: 155
fat: 0.8 g
carbohydrate: 34 g
iron: 1.5 mg (10% RNI)
calcium: 185 mg (26% RNI)

69

orange and apricot

Fresh apricots have a short season so it's important to make the most of them when they are available. They produce a deliciously sweet, luxurious tasting juice. If you can't get fresh apricots try peaches or nectarines. This juice is good during exercise as it contains plenty of calcium and iron, as well as beta-carotene, the plant form of vitamin A. Beta-carotene is essential for good vision; it also helps to fight damage caused by free radicals and can therefore protect against some cancers.

300 g (10 oz) apricots
1 large orange
300 ml (½ pint) water

Wash the apricots and remove the stones. Peel the orange and divide the flesh into segments. Juice the fruit then add the water. Pour into a glass and add ice cubes, if liked. **Makes 600 ml (1 pint); Serves 2**

Nutrition Notes

This juice is an excellent source of vitamins C, A and B6, folic acid, magnesium, phosphorus, copper and potassium and provides useful amounts of calcium and iron, making it a good, all-round choice for athletes.

Per serving

calories: 150
fat: 0.5 g
carbohydrate: 34 g
iron: 1.6 mg (11% RNI)
calcium: 116 mg (16% RNI)

71

orange, cranberry and mango

Oranges, cranberries and mangoes are packed with the antioxidant vitamin C. Women with urinary tract infections will find cranberries a good natural treatment. When fresh cranberries are not in season, use frozen cranberries instead but defrost them first.

125 g (4 oz) cranberries
1 mango
1 orange
100 ml (3½ fl oz) water
1 teaspoon clear honey

Wash the cranberries. Peel the mango and remove the stone. Peel the orange and divide the flesh into segments. Juice the fruit, pour into a glass and stir in the water and honey. Add a couple of ice cubes and drink immediately. Garnish with cranberries, if liked.
Makes 400 ml (14 fl oz); Serves 1

Nutrition Notes

This juice is an excellent source of vitamins A and C and provides useful amounts of B1, B6, copper and potassium, calcium and iron. It is a good choice before exercise as it helps to offset injury problems.

Per serving

calories: 183
fat: 0.6 g
carbohydrate: 44 g
iron: 2.1 mg (15% RNI)
calcium: 104 mg (15% RNI)

pink grapefruit
and pineapple

This is a delicious thirst-quencher in which the sweetness of the pineapple perfectly complements the more tart flavour of the pink grapefruit. It is an ideal drink during almost every type of exercise, but remember that the phytochemicals in grapefruit juice can interfere with the breakdown of certain drugs such as those used to treat high blood pressure, heart problems and asthma, increasing the risk of side effects.

1 pink grapefruit
¼ pineapple, about 215 g (7½ oz)
*   flesh, once skin and core have*
*   been removed*
300 ml (½ pint) water

Peel the grapefruit and divide the flesh into segments. Remove the skin and hard central core from the pineapple and slice the flesh into even-sized pieces. Juice the fruit then add the water. Pour into a glass and add a couple of ice cubes. **Makes 600 ml (1 pint); Serves 2**

Nutrition Notes

This juice is an excellent source of vitamins C and B6, folic acid, copper and potassium, as well as providing useful amounts of calcium.

Per serving

calories: 140
fat: 0.6 g
carbohydrate: 33 g
iron: 0.6 mg (4% RNI)
calcium: 77 mg (11% RNI)

75

strawberry and kiwifruit

Packed with vitamin C, this juice is great during exercise, as vitamin C is thought to increase oxygen uptake and aerobic energy production. Kiwifruits are also a good source of potassium, which is needed for nerve and muscle function.

150 g (5 oz) strawberries
2 kiwifruits

Wash and hull the strawberries. Peel the kiwifruits and slice them into even-sized pieces. Juice the fruit, pour it into a glass then add a couple of ice cubes, if liked.
Makes 300 ml (½ pint); Serves 1

Nutrition Notes

This juice is an excellent source of vitamin C, potassium, copper, magnesium and phosphorus, making it a good choice during exercise, when the body needs to maintain high levels of nutrients for performance.

Per serving

calories: 100
fat: 0.8 g
carbohydrate: 22 g
iron: 1 mg (7% RNI)
calcium: 54 mg (8% RNI)

strawberry, peach and apple

This juice provides useful amounts of iron, which is an important mineral for all athletes, particularly women, as it aids the transport of oxygen around the body. A deficiency in iron can adversely affect performance, both in training and competition.

125 g (4 oz) strawberries
2 peaches
1 red apple
300 ml (½ pint) water

Wash and hull the strawberries. Wash the peaches and apple. Remove the stones from the peaches. Chop the fruit into even-sized chunks and juice it. Add the water, then pour the juice into a glass and add a couple of ice cubes, if liked. **Makes 600 ml (1 pint); Serves 2**

Nutrition Notes

This juice is an excellent source of vitamin C, copper, potassium, magnesium and phosphorus. It also contains useful amounts of iron.

Per serving

calories: 153
fat: 0.4 g
carbohydrate: 36 g
iron: 1.5 mg (17% RNI)
calcium: 39 mg (5% RNI)

81

grape and kiwifruit

Kiwifruits are an excellent source of vitamin C. When choosing them select ones that are firm to the touch but not rock hard. This juice is a good choice before an endurance event such as rowing as it contains large amounts of carbohydrate for energy release, plus a hefty amount of vitamin C, to protect against muscle soreness and injury. Vitamin C may also help to increase oxygen uptake and aerobic energy production.

2 kiwifruits
300 g (10 oz) seedless green grapes

Peel the kiwifruits, chop them into even-sized pieces and juice them with the grapes. Pour the juice into a glass and add a couple of ice cubes. Garnish with grapes, if liked. **Makes 300 ml (½ pint); Serves 1**

Nutrition Notes

This juice is an excellent source of vitamins C, B1 and B6, copper, potassium, magnesium and phosphorus and also provides useful amounts of calcium.

Per serving

calories: 240
fat: 0.9 g
carbohydrate: 59 g
iron: 1.4 mg (9% RNI)
calcium: 69 mg (10% RNI)

83

grape and plum

Choose this juice before any endurance, extra-energy or general fitness activity. It is a good source of potassium, vitamin E and iron. Potassium enhances muscle and nerve function, while vitamin E is a powerful antioxidant, protecting against free radical damage and so protecting against some cancers. Iron prevents fatigue and anaemia and can positively affect performance. Interestingly, red grapes contain more antioxidant than green ones.

150 g (5 oz) seedless red grapes
5 plums, about 300 g (10 oz)

Wash the grapes and plums. Remove the stones from the plums then cut the flesh into even-sized pieces. Juice the fruit, pour it into a glass and add a couple of ice cubes. Decorate with slices of plum, if liked.
Makes 300 ml (½ pint); Serves 1

Nutrition Notes

This juice is an excellent source of vitamins A, C and B1, niacin, B6, copper and potassium, and also provides useful amounts of iron.

Per serving

calories: 190
fat: 0.5 g
carbohydrate: 48 g
iron: 1.6 mg (11% RNI)
calcium: 56 mg (8% RNI)

85

banana and peanut butter smoothie

Peanut butter may sound an unusual ingredient in a smoothie, but in fact it combines wonderfully well with bananas to make a rich, satisfying drink. Peanuts contain resveratrol, plant sterols and other phytochemicals which, according to research, have cardio-protective and cancer-inhibiting properties. This high-calcium drink is a great pick-me-up after exercise.

1 ripe banana
300 ml (½ pint) semi-skimmed milk
1 tablespoon smooth peanut butter or
 2 teaspoons tahini paste

Peel and slice the banana, put it in a freezer container and freeze for at least 2 hours or overnight. Put the banana, milk and peanut butter or tahini paste in a food processor or blender and process until smooth. Serve immediately. **Makes 400 ml (14 fl oz); Serves 1**

Nutrition Notes

Tahini is a delicious paste made from crushed sesame seeds. Weight for weight, sesame seeds contain ten times more calcium than milk. This smoothie is an excellent source of vitamins C, B1, B2, B6 and B12, folic acid, niacin, calcium, copper, potassium, zinc, magnesium and phosphorus.

Per serving

calories: 326

fat: 13 g

carbohydrate: 40 g

protein: 14 g

iron: 0.8 mg (5% RNI)

calcium: 372 mg (53% RNI)

banana, strawberry and orange smoothie

It is important that exercisers start to refuel their muscle glycogen as soon as possible after exercise and so this high-carbohydrate, low-fat smoothie is a great choice. Bananas are high in potassium, a vital mineral for muscle and nerve function, which also helps to regulate blood pressure.

1 small ripe banana
75 g (3 oz) strawberries
250 ml (8 fl oz) orange juice

Peel and slice the banana. Wash, hull and roughly chop the strawberries. Place the fruit into a freezer container and freeze for at least 2 hours or overnight. Place the frozen fruit and the orange juice in a food processor or blender and process until thick. Decorate with strawberries, if liked, and serve immediately.
Makes 400 ml (14 fl oz); Serves 1

Nutrition Notes

This smoothie is an excellent source of vitamins C, B1 and B6, folic acid, potassium, magnesium and phosphorus.

Per serving

calories: 200
fat: 0.4 g
carbohydrate: 48 g
protein: 4 g
iron: 1.3 mg (9% RNI)
calcium: 48 mg (7% RNI)

91

avocado and banana smoothie

This smoothie is suitable before carrying out low-intensity and general fitness activities. Bananas provide carbohydrate and energy, while avocados supply the body with healthy unsaturated fats. Drinking this will help to fuel the body and maintain good energy levels. Using skimmed milk helps keep down the overall fat content.

1 small ripe avocado
1 small ripe banana
250 ml (8 fl oz) skimmed milk

Peel the avocado, remove the stone and roughly chop the flesh. Peel and slice the banana. Place the avocado, banana and milk in a food processor or blender and process until smooth. Pour into a glass, add a couple of ice cubes and drink immediately.
Makes 400 ml (14 fl oz); Serves 1

Nutrition Notes

In the tropics, avocados are often called poor man's butter because of their creamy texture and high fat content. Unlike butter, though, most of the fat is monounsaturated – the sort that helps lower levels of the 'bad' cholesterol (or low-density lipoproteins) while raising levels of the 'good' cholesterol (or high-density lipoproteins). Just one avocado provides around half the recommended daily intake of vitamin B6. This smoothie is an excellent source of vitamins C, E, B1, B2, B6 and B12, as well as folic acid, calcium, potassium, copper, zinc, magnesium and phosphorus.

Per serving

calories: 270
fat: 20 g
carbohydrate: 37 g
protein: 11 g
iron: 0.85 mg (6% RNI)
calcium: 317 mg (45% RNI)

93

banana and almond smoothie

The combination of bananas, ground almonds and soya milk makes this a highly nutritious drink. Bananas are a very popular source of carbohydrate among endurance athletes, and they can be eaten before, during or after exercise, making them hugely versatile. It is best to use very ripe bananas (very yellow skin with black spots) as less ripe ones are largely indigestible.

2 very ripe bananas
450 ml (¾ pint) soya milk
40 g (1½ oz) ground almonds
pinch of ground cinnamon
a little honey (optional)

Peel and slice the bananas, put them into a freezer container and freeze for at least 2 hours or overnight. Place the frozen bananas, soya milk, ground almonds and cinnamon in a food processor or blender, add the honey, if using, and process until thick and frothy. Pour into glasses and serve immediately with ice cubes and flaked almonds. **Makes 600 ml (1 pint); Serves 2**

Nutrition Notes

Almonds are an excellent source of vitamin E as well as the minerals calcium, magnesium, phosphorus and copper. They also help to increase the protein content of this drink, which is an excellent source of vitamins C, E, B1, B2 and B6, niacin, folic acid, copper, potassium, zinc, magnesium, phosphorus and provides useful amounts of calcium.

Per serving

calories: 330
fat: 15 g
carbohydrate: 34 g
protein: 12 g
iron: 1.8 mg (13% RNI)
calcium: 85 mg (12% RNI)

summer berry smoothie

Summer berries are packed with vitamin C and B vitamins. They have a deep colour and rich flavour and so are ideal for making smoothies. Nutritionally, frozen fruit is every bit as good as fresh, and it is available all year round. Soya milk is a good alternative to cows' milk for those who are lactose-intolerant, but look for a calcium-enriched brand for maximum nutrition. This smoothie is isotonic and so may be consumed during sport, particularly low-intensity and low-impact exercises.

150 g (5 oz) frozen mixed summer berries
300 ml (½ pint) vanilla-flavoured soya milk
1 teaspoon clear honey (optional)

Place the berries, soya milk and honey, if using, in a food processor or blender and process until thick. Serve immediately decorated with berries, if liked.

Makes 400 ml (14 fl oz): Serves 1

Nutrition Notes

This drink is an excellent source of vitamins C, B1, B2 and B6, folic acid, copper, potassium, zinc, magnesium and phosphorus, and provides useful amounts of calcium and iron. It is a good, all-round smoothie for general fitness activities.

Per serving

calories: 160
fat: 6 g
carbohydrate: 18 g
protein: 10 g
iron: 2.2 mg (15% RNI)
calcium: 80 mg (11% RNI)

99

peach and orange smoothie

This delicious smoothie is ideal during endurance events or after most activities, particularly when fluid replacement is a priority. Exercise, with adequate calcium intake, helps prevent bone loss and the yogurt provides a good source of calcium.

400 g (13 oz) can peaches in
  natural juice, drained
150 g (5 oz) peach or apricot yogurt
200 ml (7 fl oz) orange juice
a little honey (optional)

Place the peaches in a food processor or blender with the yogurt, orange juice and honey, if using, and process until smooth. Add a couple of ice cubes, if liked and drink immediately. **Makes 500 ml (17 fl oz); Serves 2**

Nutrition Notes

This smoothie is an excellent source of vitamins C, B1, B2 and B6, folic acid, calcium, potassium and phosphorus, making it an ideal drink after almost any exercise.

Per serving

calories: 170
fat: 2 g
carbohydrate: 34 g
protein: 6 g
iron: 1.2 mg (8% RNI)
calcium: 170 mg (25% RNI)

101

prune, apple and cinnamon smoothie

This smoothie is rich in carbohydrate, which makes it an excellent way to replenish muscle and liver glycogen stores after exercise. This is particularly helpful in extra-energy, endurance and muscular strength activities where muscle glycogen stores are likely to be depleted. Prunes are a useful source of iron, especially for female and vegetarian athletes, and prune juice is a good alternative if you dislike eating whole prunes. As prunes are renowned for their laxative qualities, it might be wise to avoid drinking this juice before exercise.

65 g (2½ oz) ready-to-eat prunes
pinch of ground cinnamon
350 ml (12 fl oz) apple juice
3 tablespoons Greek yogurt

Roughly chop the prunes into small pieces. Put the prunes and cinnamon in a large bowl. Pour over the apple juice, cover and allow to stand overnight. Place the prunes, apple juice and yogurt in a food processor or blender and process until smooth. Pour into a glass, add ice cubes, sprinkle with cinnamon and drink immediately. **Makes 400 ml (14 fl oz); Serves 1**

Nutrition Notes

This smoothie is an excellent source of vitamins C, B2 and B6, potassium, magnesium and phosphorus and provides useful amounts of calcium and iron.

Per serving

calories: 270
fat: 5 g
carbohydrate: 56 g
protein: 5 g
iron: 2 mg (14% RNI)
calcium: 112 mg (16% RNI)

103

rhubarb and custard smoothie

Rhubarb is a great source of potassium and also contains vitamin C and manganese. However, it should form only a small part of an athlete's diet as it also contains oxalic acid, which can inhibit the absorption of calcium and iron. The custard and milk ensure that this smoothie is calcium-rich, which will offset the negative effect of oxalic acid.

150 g (5 oz) can rhubarb
150 g (5 oz) carton ready-made
   custard
100 ml (3½ fl oz) ice-cold
   semi-skimmed milk
1 teaspoon icing sugar (optional)

Drain the rhubarb then put it into a food processor or blender with the custard, milk and icing sugar, if using, and process until smooth. Pour into a glass, add a couple of ice cubes, if liked, and serve immediately. **Makes 400 ml (14 fl oz); Serves 1**

Nutrition Notes

This smoothie is an excellent source of B2, B12, calcium and phosphorus. Semi-skimmed milk contains as much calcium as full-fat milk, but has fewer calories, so it is useful for those who are watching their weight.

Per serving

calories: 135
fat: 4 g
carbohydrate: 21 g
protein: 5 g
iron: 0.7 mg (5% RNI)
calcium: 185 mg (26% RNI)

cucumber and mint lassi

Refreshing and summery, this smoothie is based on the Indian drink lassi. It contains a large amount of calcium, essential for bone health, while the cucumber's high water content makes it a good choice for quenching the thirst after activity. As it is isotonic it is easily absorbed and ideal when glycogen refuelling is not the priority.

½ cucumber, about 200 g (7 oz)
250 g (8 oz) natural bio yogurt
handful of chopped mint
¼ teaspoon salt (optional)

Slice the cucumber in half lengthways and, using a teaspoon, remove and discard the seeds. Roughly chop the flesh and place it in a food processor or blender with the yogurt, mint and salt, if using, and process until smooth. Pour into a glass, add a couple of ice cubes, decorate with mint, if liked, and drink immediately. **Makes 300 ml (½ pint); Serves 1**

Nutrition Notes

This smoothie is an excellent source of vitamins A, C, B1, B2, B6 and B12, folic acid, potassium, zinc, magnesium, phosphorus and calcium – it is good after most sports.

Per serving

calories: 220
fat: 8 g
carbohydrate: 22 g
protein: 15 g
iron: 0.8 mg (6% RNI)
calcium: 536 mg (76% RNI)

107

apricot and pineapple smoothie

Dried apricots have an increased concentration of beta-carotene, potassium and iron, making them especially useful for athletes. Drunk after exercise, this smoothie helps to refuel the muscles and helps to boost energy levels that may have been depleted, particularly after endurance activities such as long-distance running.

65 g (2½ oz) ready-to-eat dried apricots
350 ml (12 fl oz) pineapple juice

Roughly chop the apricots into small pieces and put them in a large bowl. Pour the pineapple juice over them, cover the bowl and allow to stand overnight. Tip the contents of the bowl into a food processor or blender and process until smooth. Add a couple of ice cubes and drink immediately. **Makes 350 ml (12 fl oz); Serves 1**

Nutrition Notes

Dried apricots are a useful source of calcium particularly for anyone on a dairy-free diet. Many brands of dried apricots are preserved using sulphur dioxide, which can trigger asthma attacks. To avoid this, check the packaging before you buy, or rinse the apricots well before eating them. This smoothie is an excellent source of vitamins C, B1 and B6, copper, potassium, magnesium and phosphorus and provides useful amounts of calcium and iron.

Per serving

calories: 240
fat: 0.7 g
carbohydrate: 59 g
protein: 3.5 g
iron: 2.7 mg (18% RNI)
calcium: 72 mg (10% RNI)

cranberry and mango smoothie

Containing high levels of carbohydrate for energy, and calcium for bone health and strength, this smoothie is ideal for many athletes. Cranberry juice is a natural way of fighting urinary tract infections, which can blight training and performance for female athletes in particular.

1 ripe mango
200 ml (7 fl oz) cranberry juice
150 g (5 oz) peach yogurt

Peel the mango, remove the stone and roughly chop the flesh. Place the flesh in a food processor or blender with the cranberry juice and yogurt and process until smooth. Pour into a glass, add a couple of ice cubes, decorate with slices of mango, if liked, and drink immediately. **Makes 400 ml (14 fl oz); Serves 1**

Nutrition Notes

This smoothie is an excellent source of vitamins A, C, B1, B2, B6 and B12, folic acid, calcium, zinc, potassium, magnesium and phosphorus and also provides useful amounts of iron.

Per serving

calories: 280
fat: 5 g
carbohydrate: 52 g
protein: 10 g
iron: 1.4 mg (10% RNI)
calcium: 332 mg (47% RNI)

orange, mango and strawberry smoothie

As it contains useful amounts of calcium, iron and carbohydrate and has low fat levels, this smoothie is perfect after endurance events or for athletes who practise exercises such as weight-training. This is because it replaces energy and raises iron levels, while also helping to maintain bone health.

125 g (4 oz) strawberries
1 small ripe mango
300 ml (½ pint) orange juice

Wash and hull the strawberries, place them in a freezer container and freeze for 2 hours or overnight. Peel the mango, remove the stone, roughly chop the flesh and place in a food processor or blender with the strawberries and orange juice and process until thick. Decorate with slices of orange, if liked, and serve immediately. **Makes 400 ml (14 fl oz); Serves 1**

Nutrition Notes

This smoothie is an excellent source of vitamins A, C, B1, B2 and B6, folic acid, copper, potassium, magnesium and phosphorus and also provides useful amounts of calcium and iron.

Per serving

calories: 230
fat: 0.7 g
carbohydrate: 55 g
protein: 3.5 g
iron: 2.1 mg (14% RNI)
calcium: 68 mg (10% RNI)

tropical fruit
smoothie

Versatility is the key to this smoothie. It is likely to be well absorbed, as it is isotonic, and provides a good source of carbohydrate to fuel activity and refuel afterwards. It is also a very good source of calcium, which is essential for bone health and strength. Bananas and mangoes also supply fibre, making this a filling and satisfying smoothie.

1 large banana
1 large ripe mango
150 g (5 oz) natural bio yogurt
300 ml (½ pint) pineapple juice

Peel and slice the banana, then put it in a freezer container and freeze for at least 2 hours or overnight. Peel the mango, remove the stone and roughly chop the flesh. Place it in a food processor or blender with the frozen banana, yogurt and pineapple juice. Process until smooth and serve immediately, decorated with pineapple chunks, if liked. **Makes 600 ml (1 pint); Serves 2**

Nutrition Notes

This smoothie is an excellent source of vitamins A, C, B1, B2 and B6, folic acid, calcium, potassium, copper, magnesium and phosphorus. Adding yogurt to a smoothie is an effective way to increase its calcium content.

Per serving

calories: 230
fat: 2.8 g
carbohydrate: 48 g
protein: 6 g
iron: 1.1 mg (8% RNI)
calcium: 176 mg (25% RNI)

kiwifruit, melon and passion fruit smoothie

This is a deliciously sweet, yet refreshing drink. If you cannot find passion fruit juice try using pineapple juice instead. This smoothie is beneficial after most exercise, particularly extra-energy, endurance and muscular strength activities, when muscle glycogen stores are often quickly used up.

¼ **watermelon, about 300 g (10 oz) flesh**
2 kiwifruits
200 ml (7 fl oz) passion fruit juice

Remove and discard the seeds from the watermelon and dice the flesh. Put it in a freezer container and freeze for at least 2 hours or overnight. Peel and roughly chop the kiwifruits and place them in a food processor or blender with the watermelon and the passion fruit juice and process until thick. Serve immediately. **Makes 400 ml (14 fl oz); Serves 1**

Nutrition Notes

This smoothie is an excellent source of vitamins A, C, B1, B2 and B6, copper, potassium, zinc, magnesium and phosphorus and provides useful amounts of iron and calcium. Its wealth of nutrients makes it perfect after a wide range of exercise and sports.

Per serving

calories: 250
fat: 1.7 g
carbohydrate: 55 g
protein: 4.5 g
iron: 2.4 mg (18% RNI)
calcium: 65 mg (10% RNI)

119

banana and mango smoothie

Supplying good amounts of carbohydrate and potassium for nerve and muscle function, bananas are a popular snack among endurance athletes. They also contain a type of fibre, fructoligosaccharides (FOS), which encourage the growth of friendly lactobacilli bacteria in the gut. These help prevent the overgrowth of bad bacteria, which can cause health problems, such as digestive disorders.

1 ripe banana
1 ripe mango
200 ml (7 fl oz) orange juice
200 ml (7 fl oz) semi-skimmed milk
3 tablespoons fromage frais

Peel and slice the banana. Peel the mango, remove the stone and cut the flesh into even-sized pieces. Put the banana, mango, orange juice, milk and fromage frais in a food processor or blender and process until smooth. Pour into 2 glasses, add a couple of ice cubes to each glass if liked, and drink immediately.
Makes 500 ml (17 fl oz); Serves 2

Nutrition Notes

This smoothie is an excellent source of vitamins A, C, B1, B2, B6 and B12, folic acid, calcium, potassium, magnesium and phosphorus.

Per serving

calories: 190
fat: 3 g
carbohydrate: 37 g
protein: 6 g
iron: 0.95 mg (6% RNI)
calcium: 155 mg (22% RNI)

121

strawberry and pineapple smoothie

Like many smoothies, this one is a great way of restoring energy after exercise, when solid food may not appeal. It contains a high level of calcium, which is essential for healthy bones, helps to maintain normal blood pressure and plays a role in nerve transmission, muscle contraction and blood clotting – all of which are crucial bodily functions for athletes.

150 g (5 oz) strawberries
150 ml (¼ pint) pineapple juice
150 g (5 oz) strawberry yogurt

Wash, hull and roughly chop the strawberries, then place them in a freezer container and freeze for at least 2 hours or overnight. Place the frozen strawberries, pineapple juice and yogurt in a food processor or blender and process until smooth. Pour into a glass, add a couple of ice cubes, decorate with strawberries, if liked, and drink immediately.
Makes 400 ml (14 fl oz); Serves 1

Nutrition Notes

This smoothie is an excellent source of vitamins C, B2 and B6, folic acid, calcium, zinc, magnesium and phosphorus.

Per serving

calories: 260
fat: 4.5 g
carbohydrate: 48 g
protein: 9 g
iron: 0.9 mg (6% RNI)
calcium: 276 mg (39% RNI)

123

dried fruit salad smoothie

This excellent smoothie allows athletes to refuel and increase their energy levels after endurance activities and extra-energy sports, which can leave people feeling drained and hungry. Dried fruit provides a source of iron, so this is a good choice for those who are at risk of iron deficiency and those practising impact sports.

125 g (4 oz) dried fruit salad
400 ml (14 fl oz) apple juice,
  more if necessary
200 ml (7 fl oz) Greek yogurt

Roughly chop the fruit and place it in a large bowl. Pour the apple juice over it, cover the bowl and allow to stand overnight. Put the dried fruit salad and apple juice in a food processor or blender, add the yogurt and process until smooth, adding a little more apple juice if necessary. Pour into 2 glasses, add a couple of ice cubes, if liked, and serve immediately. **Makes 450 ml (¾ pint); Serves 2**

Nutrition Notes

This smoothie is an excellent source of vitamins A, C, B2, B6 and B12, calcium, potassium, magnesium and phosphorus and also provides useful amounts of iron.

Per serving

calories: 280
fat: 8 g
carbohydrate: 48 g
protein: 7 g
iron: 2.3 mg (15% RNI)
calcium: 200 mg (29% RNI)

125

glossary

Antioxidant: A compound that protects cells against the damaging effects of free radicals. Vitamins C, E, beta-carotene and selenium and many of the phytochemicals found in fruit and vegetables act as antioxidants.

Carbohydrate: A primary energy fuel for the body.

Enzyme: A protein that speeds up chemical reactions and processes in the body.

Ergogenic aid: A substance that is capable of enhancing work performance.

Essential fatty acids: These are polyunsaturated fatty acids, which cannot be made by the body and so must be supplied by food. The main sources of essential fatty acids (also called linoleic and linolenic acids) are olive and vegetable oils, fish oils, polyunsaturated margarine and nuts.

Fibre: Also called non-starch polysaccharides (NSP), this is the word used to describe several different compounds found in the cell walls of all plants. The body cannot digest fibre but nevertheless it plays an important role in our health. Fibre can be divided into two groups – see Soluble fibre and Insoluble fibre

Free radicals: These are highly reactive molecules which cause damage to cell walls and DNA (the genetic material found within cells). They are believed to be involved in the development of heart disease, some cancers and premature ageing. Free radicals are produced naturally but certain factors such as smoking, pollution and exposure to sunlight can accelerate their production.

Fructoligosaccharides (FOS): A type of fibre that escapes the digestive process and is fermented by the bacteria in the gut. FOS encourage the growth of 'friendly' lactobacilli bacteria in the gut.

Glycaemic index (GI): A measure of how quickly carbohydrate is turned into blood glucose. Foods with a high GI are quickly broken down and provide a fast energy fix, whilst those with a low GI are absorbed more slowly and steadily into the blood. Unfortunately, there is no easy way to tell what the GI of a food is. Some sugars have a high GI and others a low GI. Some complex carbohydrates have a low GI whereas others have a higher GI. Foods that have a low glycaemic index include beans, pulses, apples, pears, pasta, dried apricots and wholewheat cereals. Foods with a high glycaemic index include honey, baked potatoes, glucose, white rice, bagels and watermelons.

Glycogen: The main carbohydrate store in the body, stored mainly in the liver and muscles.

Insoluble fibre: Found in wholegrain cereals, pulses, fruit and vegetables, insoluble fibre increases stool bulk and speeds the passage of waste material through the body. It helps prevent constipation, haemorrhoids, diverticular disease and may protect against bowel cancer.

Macronutrients: Nutrients that are present in foods in large quantities; they include fats, proteins and carbohydrates.

Micronutrients: Nutrients that are present in foods in small quantities; they include vitamins and minerals.

Minerals: Inorganic substances that perform a wide range of vital functions throughout the body.

Phytochemicals: Naturally occurring compounds that plants produce to protect themselves against bacteria, viruses and fungi. They are not nutrients in the true sense of the word because they are not essential in the diet, but they are biologically active and there is a growing amount of evidence to suggest that they can help protect against various types of cancer, heart disease, and chronic degenerative diseases like cataracts and arthritis.

Reference Nutrient Intakes (RNIs): This refers to the amount of a particular nutrient which is sufficient to meet the nutritional needs of most individuals. The figures are published by the Department of Health and vary depending on age, sex and specific nutritional needs such as pregnancy. They are equivalent to what used to be called Recommended Daily Amounts or Intakes (RDA/RDI).

Soluble fibre: This is found in oats, beans and pulses, fruit and vegetables and can help reduce high blood cholesterol levels and control blood sugar levels by slowing down the absorption of sugar.

Vitamins: A group of compounds, required in minute amounts, but essential for good health. There are about 20 vitamins, most of which cannot be made by the body and must therefore be obtained from the diet. Each vitamin performs one or several essential functions within the body. The body can store some vitamins (A, D, E, K and B12); the rest need to be provided regularly by the diet.

index

127

Acknowledgements

The author and publisher would like to thank PPL
(tel: 01159 608646, www.superjuicer.co.uk) for
the loan of the Superjuicer, and Magimix for the
loan of Le Duo juicer.

Executive editor Nicky Hill
Editor Sharon Ashman
Executive art editor Geoff Fennell
Production controller Jo Sim
Photographer Karen Thomas
Home economist David Morgan
Stylist Angela Swaffield
Illustrations Line + Line